THE PSYCHOLOG
Wales: On

Phil Williams

THE GREGYNOG PAPERS
Volume Three • Number Three

Welsh Academic Press

Published in Wales by Welsh Academic Press, an imprint of

Ashley Drake Publishing Ltd
PO Box 733
Cardiff
CF14 2YX

First Impression – 2003

ISBN
1 86057 0666

©Institute of Welsh Affairs / Prof. Phil Williams

British Library Cataloguing-in-Publication Data.
A CIP catalogue for this book is available from the British Library.

THE AUTHOR – Professor Phil Williams

The late Professor Phil Williams was Plaid Cymru's AM for South Wales East during the first term of the National Assembly, 1999-2003, when he served on the Economic Development and European Committees. Born in Tredegar in 1939, Professor Williams grew up in Bargoed, was educated at Lewis School, Pengam, and Clare College, Cambridge, where he completed a Ph.D. in radio astronomy. He became a professor in the Physics Department at the University of Wales, Aberystwyth, in 1992, specialising in Solar Terrestrial Physics.

The Institute of Welsh Affairs exists to promote quality research and informed debate affecting the cultural, social, political and economic well-being of Wales. IWA is an independent organisation owing no allegiance to any political or economic interest group. Our only interest is in seeing Wales flourish as a country in which to work and live. We are funded by a range of organisations and individuals. For more information about the Institute, its publications, and how to join, either as an individual or corporate supporter, contact:

IWA – Institute of Welsh Affairs
Ty Oldfield
Llantrisant Road
Llandâf
Cardiff
CF5 2YQ

Tel 029 2057 5511
Fax 029 2057 5701
Email wales@iwa.org.uk
Web www.iwa.org.uk

CONTENTS

PREFACE

The completion of the National Assembly's first term was an opportune moment to consider, not just its record in terms of the policies and new directions of expenditure that have resulted, but its wider impact on the life and culture of the nation. This, in essence is what this Paper seeks to do. It concludes that the Assembly has the potential to create a unified civic culture in the face of many divisive tendencies and sometimes a fractured sensibility that so often characterises the Welsh identity.

The Paper utilises the concept of 'the psychology of distance' to explore the cross currents of division that challenge our policy makers in the Assembly Government. The most quoted divide in Wales is between north and south. Yet there are great similarities between these two halves of the country. The distance between them is largely psychological, simply because their peoples so seldom meet. In respect of other divides, for instance between the poorer communities of Wales and those that are more prosperous, the physical distance is often very small. As Professor Williams points out, Cyncoed in Cardiff, by a large measure the least deprived ward in Wales, is less than 20 miles from the Gurnos estate in Merthyr, which is one of the most deprived parts of the country. Yet, as he says, the "psychological barriers can be just as daunting as the barriers of distance." For the long-term unemployed living in impoverished communities such as Gurnos the prosperous parts of Cardiff must seem a million miles away: "In these matters of relative separation the psychology of distance is truly at work." Without being fully conscious of such divisions we will have no chance of addressing them.

This is the tenth Paper that has arisen out of a seminar held at the Gregynog University of Wales Conference Centre near Newtown, Powys. Each seminar comprises around ten people including the author and the editor. They meet for dinner and an opening presentation by the author during a weekend evening and stay overnight. The seminar then continues the following day.

The seminar out of which this Paper has been produced was held in early November 2002. In addition to Professor Williams and myself, those attending were: Professor Jane Aaron, of the University of Glamorgan; Graham Day, of the University of Wales, Bangor; Geraint Talfan Davies, Chair of the IWA; Angela Elniff-Larsen, Director of Community Enterprise Wales; Eurfyl ap Gwilym, a business consultant; Rhys Jones, of the University of Wales, Aberystwyth; David Melding, Conservative AM for South Wales Central; Professor Peter Stead, of the University of Glamorgan; and Elin Royles, of the University of Wales, Aberystwyth. All contributed extensively to the discussions. However, responsibility for the contents of this published Paper is the responsibility of the author alone.

Sadly, while this Paper was in production we received the news that its author had died, suddenly, in Cardiff on 10 June 2003. Only a week or so before Phil had delivered the final, corrected proofs to the IWA office. "If you gave me more time I could add more," he said. "But I'm pretty happy with the way it is." We went on to discuss what might be on the cover of the publication, an issue we left undecided, save to say it should not be yet another map of Wales. As it is that decision has made itself. In his own varied and brilliant life, Phil Williams resolved many of the tensions, contradictions and paradoxes that resonate in the country he loved so much and which he addressed in this Paper in terms of 'the psychology of distance'.

John Osmond
Director, Institute of Welsh Affairs
June 2003

INTRODUCTION

I write this when the identity of Wales as a separate nation is stronger than at any time in my life. The establishment of the National Assembly is obviously the most significant single change. It is associated with the growing status of the Welsh language, the emergence of Welsh civic society, and the willingness of over two-thirds of the resident population to identify themselves as primarily Welsh.

This is a remarkable development and sometimes I pinch myself to prove that it is not a dream. When I was a child during the Second World War it would be fair to say that, however the identity of Wales was measured, the relevant characteristics would have shown a steady decline throughout the twentieth century: the proportion of the population born in Wales, the proportion speaking Welsh, the proportion who were members of a Welsh church and probably – though there are few measurements of this – the proportion regarding themselves as Welsh rather than British. If my memory serves me right, in the public celebrations at the end of the war there were far more Union Jacks than Red Dragons.

In the 1940s most people would have assumed this trend would continue, linked as it was with the obvious strength of those forces that divided Wales and the apparent weakness of those forces that defended the unity of Wales. In fact the reverse has happened. The results of the 2001 census show – for the first time since 1911 – an increase in the number of people able to speak Welsh. A large number of voluntary bodies have recently re-organised to establish – in theory at least – separate and distinct parts of each organisation covering Wales.

Moreover, the existence of Wales as a separate nation is, at last, officially recognised. Of course this is within a UK context. We now have a Lord Chief Justice of England and Wales and even an England and Wales Cricket Board, though this is still referred to as the ECB.

The important semantic advance was the designation of our new legislature as the 'National Assembly for Wales'. There are some people who think that since Scotland has a 'Scottish Parliament' and Wales a 'National Assembly' this represents a lower status. However, if we look at the 191 members of the United Nations we see that far-and-away the most common name for the highest elected legislature in an independent country is 'National Assembly', the title chosen by 57 of the UN member states, with only 15 choosing 'Parliament'.

This has redefined the exact meaning of the word 'national' in Westminster legislation. As a result, the word is used, even by the UK Government and by Government bodies, to refer to Wales (or, of course, to England or Scotland), and the BBC frequently refers to 'the nations and regions of the United Kingdom'.

Yet confusion remains. When reference is made in the press to the 'national average' it is not only my Welsh sensitivities that are alerted: my passion for statistical accuracy wants to know whether the figures apply to Wales, or to England-and-Wales, or to Britain, or to the UK. The fact is that to many people in England the terms England, Britain, UK and even the British Isles are more-or-less synonymous. The confusion between Britain and UK is universal. A friend in East Anglia was once offered promotion provided he was prepared to work anywhere in Britain. As he knew I cared about these things he asked me whether Britain included Northern Ireland. I confirmed that it didn't but warned him that his employers might not realise this.

As we might expect from the Census fiasco, the Office of National (sic) Statistics is especially confused. On the web-page describing 'Administrative Geography' the link 'Countries of the UK' tells us there is a 'national' government at Westminster but on the very same page the link 'Wales' refers to a 'national' assembly in Wales.

Ambiguity and confusion pervade the ONS. Under the schedule for publication of Department for Education

National Statistics 'national' refers, quite properly, to England. Under the heading 'Key census statistics for local authorities', which presents a 'complex picture of the nation', the nation in question is that strange composite 'England and Wales'. But, in the report on below-average earnings the reference to a 'national average' applies to Britain – or England, Wales and Scotland. The Claimant Count in the Labour Market Assessment also refers to Britain. However, in the same Labour Assessment, Hours Worked and Unemployment Rate refer to the UK – or England, Wales, Scotland and Northern Ireland. There is clearly a long way to go before Whitehall genuinely accepts that the word 'national' can only be properly applied to Wales, England, Scotland or Ireland.

At least these are proper names: United Kingdom is only a constitutional description, and whereas more and more people refer to themselves as Welsh I have never yet found anyone owning up to being UKish. There are some who regard themselves as British, but with the disappearance of the British Empire this is a declining minority.

In the light of all this confusion it is remarkable that in answer to a new question in the Labour Force survey 69.2 per cent of the residents of Wales regard themselves primarily as Welsh. The proportion among residents born in Wales is much higher. Despite everything it is the single identity of Wales that is ascendant.

So I am an optimist. In this essay I will analyse the forces that have tended to divide Wales but also the reactions within Wales that have, despite everything, preserved an unexpected degree of nationhood and national unity. Then I would like to make a few predictions of how the balance is changing and suggest how the National Assembly might counter the divisive tendencies and strengthen the unity.

Chapter 1

THE DIVISIONS OF WALES

A continuing theme throughout our history is that there are two very different geographic regions called north Wales and south Wales, inhabited by two different tribes – the Northwalians and the Southwalians. I remember Robyn Lewis, our present Archdruid, pointing out that although he would rather be known as Cymro than as a Welshman there was no way in which he was a Walian! Yet a generation ago a prominent Welsh poet, John Eilian, fought a Westminster election on behalf of the Conservative party insisting that the only valid 'regional' boundaries were those established in pre-Roman times. He argued that the Ordovices in the north did not share a common identity with the Silures in the south, and Liverpool was, and should continue to be, the capital of the North – giving the place a capital letter is indicative of its separateness from the rest of the country. John Eilian may have roamed the wilder territories of political debate, but there is no doubt that many people had similar prejudices. Often in the south I heard people declare that they didn't really like the people in north Wales, though in most cases they had never ventured further north than Merthyr Tydfil. Just like the Guinness advert that claimed some people hated the taste of Guinness so much they had never ever tasted it. I also remember hitch-hiking from Aberdaron when I was a student. I had a lift from a local farmer and when I told him I came from the south he responded that he had once been to Dolgellau. The psychology of distance has never been based on cartography.

So as a frontal attack on the idea that there are two very

different regions called 'North Wales' and 'South Wales', I would like to describe in some detail one of the distinct regions of Wales. It is a region bounded on two sides by sea with almost the whole population within 50 km of the coast. Nevertheless most of the land area is upland, above the 200 metre contour. The main railway line runs west-east, near the coast, as does the main dual carriageway, with both leading out of Wales.

In the west of this region Welsh has survived as a community language, but as we move towards the east the proportion of Welsh speakers drops steadily until along the border only a small percentage still speak Welsh. However, even in these areas Welsh was the predominant language two centuries ago, and throughout the region there has been a long tradition of local eisteddfodau with a parallel musical culture associated with friendly competition in both solo and choral singing. In the nineteenth and early twentieth century the religious affiliation of the region was strongly nonconformist with only a minority of the population members of the Anglican Church, a minority generally associated with English-speaking, Tory land owners.

Pastoral farming has been the traditional mainstay of the regional economy, with a limited amount of cereal production near the coast and in the flood plains of the main rivers. However, in the east of the region coal and steel became major industries, with textile manufacture as a significant third sector. These industries grew rapidly in the late eighteenth and the nineteenth century, creating communities that were strongly identified with a single industry. This was especially so in the case of the villages built within walking distance of a coalmine or a steelworks.

In the second half of the twentieth century the coal and steel industries disappeared almost totally, declining as rapidly as they had grown. Tourism has now become a very prominent sector in a mixed economy, but there are many pockets of poverty and deprivation. Finally, this region boasts a strong radical tradition in politics, springing from the powerful combination of nonconformist religion and heavy industry. Since the extension of the franchise in 1868 Tory MPs have always been a minority of the elected members. Indeed, on three occasions the region returned no Tory MPs to Westminster at all – even from those constituencies that were predominantly rural. Left-wing electoral politics has been matched on occasions by militant political and trade-union action with a strong memory of extended and bitter strikes.

By now you will have guessed the game I am playing. In every respect my description applies equally well to the north or the south. The similarities are so marked that it is a remarkable achievement of ignorance and indoctrination that so many people imagine profound differences between north and south. It must also be pointed out that when politicians like the former Caerphilly Labour MP Ness Edwards and Aneurin Bevan claimed that the miners of south Wales had more in common with the miners of Durham than with farmers in north Wales they failed to recognise, or deliberately ignored, the obvious corollary that the interlaced combination of coal miners, steel workers and farmers that made up the communities of the south had far more in common with the exact same combination in the north than with any other community on earth.

Indeed, there are only two important cultural or socio-economic differences that I can recognise. The first is the difference in the form of spoken Welsh. In the absence of 'King's Welsh', over many centuries the dialects of north and south tended to diverge, as always happens when there is no central authority to define a common standard for a language. The same, of course, happened with Irish and Breton within the Celtic world. When I lived in northern Scandinavia I discovered that the problem existed to an even greater extent with the different dialects of the Samisk language.

One of the many miracles that have contributed to the survival of Wales is that in our case the gap was filled to a remarkable extent by Bishop Morgan's translation of the Bible in 1588. Yet there was always a clear difference between the classical Welsh of the Bible and the language spoken in each locality. Over the centuries, as the spoken language developed, the differences increased with no centripetal force holding the different dialects together. As compensation this allowed the dialects themselves to retain greater literary status than is ever possible in a centralised state where only one standard form is acceptable in government circles and educated society. This process, for example, led to the disappearance of Northumbrian in England and the enfeeblement of Provençal in France.

At the same time it must be emphasised that the differences in dialect between north and south have often been exaggerated. In the textbook I used to learn Welsh the main differences in the vocabulary and grammatical forms of the two dialects are summarised in two-and-a-half pages. As the editors of the Welsh Academy English-Welsh Dictionary state authoritatively, "The differences between all the varieties of spoken Welsh concern only a tiny proportion of the vocabulary; the differences have often been exaggerated, usually out of sheer ignorance or hostility".

For better or worse, over the past 40 years the development of *Cymraeg Byw* as a standard form of spoken Welsh, the availability of bilingual versions of many official documents, the establishment of S4C, and the increasing mobility of young people in Wales have combined to eliminate the problems of communication between different dialects. There is a valid debate as to whether it is an unmitigated benefit to lower the status of local dialects. Many of the pioneers of *Cymraeg Byw* did not see it as a prescription for a single, uniform standard but as a teaching aid, acting as a bridge for learners to help them acquire full command of both the standard written syntax and a local spoken dialect. Nevertheless, the *de-facto* emergence of a standard form of the language has removed one of the presumed barriers to the unity of Wales that had divided north and south.

The second genuine difference between north and south is the fact that Liverpool, the main city that has traditionally served the north as a commercial centre, lies outside Wales whereas Cardiff, which has played a very similar rôle in the south, lies within Wales. Here too the significance of this distinction is far less than it was. Both Liverpool and Cardiff developed rapidly as ports in the nineteenth century, and both declined in the twentieth century. However, as the capital of Wales Cardiff has found a new rôle. This is best illustrated by the way in which the population of Liverpool has declined in recent years and that of Cardiff has increased. It is surely significant that the Liverpool Daily Post is now the Daily Post and edited in Llandudno Junction.

So the following question must be asked: if Wales is fundamentally divided between north and south, how is it that the two regions are so similar? Or, turning the question on its head, given such fundamental similarity in so many characteristics, why has there ever been a perceived division between north and south? Is this merely a matter of the psychology of distance?

Chapter 2

A THREE-WAY SPLIT

There is a more convincing academic case that might challenge the idea of Wales as a single nation: this proposes a three-way split between the rural Welsh-speaking areas, the English-speaking areas dependent on heavy industry, and the areas of new prosperity. In his essay 'A Question of History' Dai Smith reminded us that Sir Alfred Zimmern, who held the first chair in International Politics at the University of Wales Aberystwyth, proposed a similar three-way division of Wales as far back as 1921.[1] In a lecture in Oxford Zimmern referred to "Welsh Wales, American Wales and … upper-class, or English Wales".[2] In the early 1980s Dennis Balsom made a similar division, but to allow for the changes over 60 years, and with a sounder appreciation of the real situation throughout Wales than Zimmern could possibly have acquired, he uses the term 'Y Fro Gymraeg' to represent the Welsh-speaking areas, and with admirable boldness re-defines the term 'Welsh Wales' to describe the old industrial areas, predominantly English-speaking but often passionately 'Welsh'. (From here on I shall use this definition of 'Welsh Wales'). Finally, instead of the upper strata of all Welsh society that Zimmern christened 'English Wales', Balsom identified those areas on the coast and along the border with England, the most prosperous areas of Wales that continue to attract high levels of in-migration, as 'British Wales'.[3] In a crude way this three-way division reflects the areas of greatest support for Plaid Cymru, the Labour Party and the Conservatives / Liberal Democrats respectively.

As John Osmond points out in a recent IWA Paper, the

summary results of the 1997 referendum appear to confirm this division with one important qualification: the division between Y Fro Gymraeg and Welsh Wales is in no way as deep as between these two and British Wales.[4] In the devolution referendum, the eleven counties that cover most of British Wales voted 'No' whereas the counties of Y Fro Gymraeg and Welsh Wales voted 'Yes'. But in the level of support there was no distinction between Y Fro Gymraeg and Welsh Wales, with the most positive county result coming from Neath Port Talbot, and the six most positive results split equally. It must also be added that even the separate pattern in British Wales was not as starkly different as simple green red maps, indicating Yes and No counties, would suggest. The proportion voting 'Yes' lay between 40 per cent and 60 per cent in 15 of the 22 counties, and the total number of 'Yes' votes from Monmouthshire was sufficient to provide the overall majority in Wales with a comfortable margin to spare.

In 1999 this basic similarity between Y Fro Gymraeg and Welsh Wales was reflected in the results of the first Assembly elections, the County Council elections and the subsequent European elections. For the first time in 80 years the hegemony of Labour in Welsh Wales was seriously challenged, with Plaid Cymru winning Rhondda, Islwyn and Llanelli in the Assembly elections, and taking control of the two largest local authorities in the Valleys, Caerffili and Rhondda-Cynon-Taf, so that 46 per cent of the population in the old mining Valleys found themselves living in counties under Plaid Cymru control. Despite the set-back for Plaid Cymru in 2003 there are clear signs that the political divisions between the Welsh-speaking rural fringe and the Labour heartland in the old coal-and-steel districts are not as strong as they were. In his Paper John Osmond also refers to the links that were established between rural communities and the mining valleys during the 1983 miners' strike. It would be hard to identify and measure the long-term consequences of these links, but they certainly symbolise a far greater degree of unity within Wales than suggested by the simple three-way model.

This interpretation is further confirmed by the remarkable growth of Welsh medium education in the Valleys of the south at a time when the number of Welsh-speaking communities in Y Fro Gymraeg is declining. According to the 1997 Welsh Household Interview Survey the proportion of children between the ages of three and 16 who are able to speak Welsh is 17 per cent in Rhondda Cynon Taf and Caerffili, 22 per cent in Neath Port Talbot, and an amazing 29 per cent in Torfaen. These figures must be treated with caution. In communities where very few parents speak Welsh they may genuinely believe that their children are fluent in Welsh when this is not the case. Nevertheless, from personal experience I can confirm that the success of Welsh-medium schools in my home area of Cwm Rhymni is another of the unexpected miracles.

The summary results of the recent Census confirm this trend. The eight counties that in 1991 recorded less than 10 per cent of the population aged three-plus able to speak Welsh showed an average increase of 4.5 per cent. On the other hand the eight counties with more than 20 per cent Welsh-speaking showed an average decrease of 4.0 per cent.

The challenge is now similar in all parts of Wales. In Y Fro Gymraeg it is urgent to *retain* Welsh as a community language in the face of the out-migration of young people in search of good jobs and a corresponding in-migration of retired people from England. In the Valleys and in British Wales it will be necessary to use the statistical increase in the number of young people able to speak Welsh to *re-establish* Welsh as a community language. In both cases the challenge is to secure Welsh as a community language, so that even when we consider the rôle of language the sharp division between Y Fro Gymraeg and the rest of Wales is disappearing.

Converging attitudes are also illustrated by the recent survey published by the Office of National Statistics and referred to in the introduction. As a belated but nonetheless welcome acknowledgement of the appalling mishandling of the 'ethnic' question in the 2001 census, the latest Labour Survey includes an additional question concerning national identity. From the results we learn that the county with the highest proportion of inhabitants regarding themselves *primarily* as Welsh was Merthyr Tydfil (86.8 per cent) and the next five places in the list were also counties in the old coal-mining districts of the south. The highest proportion recorded in Y Fro Gymraeg was Carmarthenshire where 75.9 per cent of the resident population regarded themselves as Welsh.

The main reason for the primacy of Welsh Wales in these results, of course, is that the coal-mining districts have, for many decades, suffered from out-migration so that the vast majority of the population were born in Wales. In contrast, the rural areas in Y Fro Gymraeg have attracted considerable in-migration from England. Nevertheless, when the ONS Survey restricted the analysis to those members of the sample actually born in Wales, the six counties with the highest proportion of Welsh-born population considering themselves as primarily Welsh are the same six who returned the highest proportion of 'Yes' votes in the referendum, split equally between Y Fro Gymraeg and Welsh Wales. Thus a higher proportion of Welsh-born population in Merthyr regard themselves as Welsh (92.0 per cent) than in Ceredigion (91.2 per cent) and by the same measure Blaenau Gwent (89.0 per cent) regards itself as more Welsh than Anglesey (85.3 per cent).

Incidentally, two very encouraging results emerge from this survey. First, 69.2 per cent of the total sample regard themselves primarily as Welsh – well over double the total proportion that regard themselves as British, English or some other nationality. Second, the sample suggests that about 120,000 of the population born outside Wales nevertheless regard themselves as Welsh. It seems that despite all the forces of Anglicisation and globalisation, Wales is still able to assimilate a substantial proportion of those who come to Wales to live so that they identify with their country of adoption. It should be added, however, that less than half of the resident population of Flintshire (43.2 per cent) regard themselves as Welsh, an indication that only a certain level of in-migration can be assimilated automatically.

It seems therefore that the real division in modern Wales is far more west east than north south, and to a very large extent this follows the division between more- and less-prosperous regions. There is one important consequence of the conceptual way in which we divide Wales. North and south are far apart, and divided by a sparsely-populated area with poor communications. Actual contacts between individuals in north and south are infrequent without a specific reason such as an all-Wales meeting. If instead we consider the real division between the prosperous and deprived areas of Wales, the distances are often trivial. Cyncoed in Cardiff, by a large measure the least deprived ward in Wales, is less than 20 miles from the Gurnos estate in Merthyr, number 4 in the Index of Multiple Deprivation. It is unlikely that many of the residents of Cyncoed visit Gurnos, though many young people from the Valleys travel to Cardiff for work and for their social life. It must be remembered, however, that social barriers can be just as daunting as the barriers of distance. For the long-term unemployed living in impoverished communities such as Gurnos the prosperous parts of Cardiff must seem a totally alien and remote environment. Once again the psychology of distance can not be measured on road maps.

Chapter 3

OBJECTIVE 1

Debates on the conceptual division of Wales may seem very academic but in 1998 this division assumed a considerable economic significance in the context of European structural funds, and especially Objective One. According to Eurostat, the Statistical Office of the European Union, Wales as a whole is a 'NUTS 1' region (that is to say, Nomenclature of Territorial Units for Statistics, level 1). This, in turn, is divided into two 'NUTS 2' regions that until 1998 approximately represented the north and the south.

Now eligibility for the highest level of European structural funding is confined to NUTS 2 regions where the average GDP per head is less than 75 per cent the average for the EU as a whole. Using the old division, in both north and south the most deprived areas were joined with the most prosperous to give an overall NUTS 2 region that 'enjoyed' an average GDP more than 75 per cent the EU average. Thus in the north the relatively prosperous areas of Deeside and Wrecsam were combined with much poorer areas in Gwynedd to give an overall GDP per head of 82.5 per cent of the EU average, and so ineligible for Objective 1. In the south the prosperity of the coastal strip from the Vale of Glamorgan to Monmouthshire similarly outweighed the deprivation of the Valleys to give an average GDP of 78 per cent. As a result neither north nor south could qualify for Objective 1 funding.[5]

I will leave it to historians to judge whether it was a preconceived idea of the natural division of Wales into north and south among Government and civil servants, plus indolence and indifference, that were responsible for this unfortunate situation before 1998, or whether it was a deliberate choice by Ministers in the Government of that time. Following the famous Fontainebleau agreement, where Mrs Thatcher hand-bagged her way to a special rebate on the UK contribution to the EU, the Conservative Administration certainly recognised that for every £3 million in structural funds from the EU earmarked for projects in Wales the Treasury would lose £2 million in direct rebate, and would also be under pressure to contribute a further £3 million in 'match-funding'. If such funds were approved and 'match-funding' allocated by the government, the UK as a whole would be £1 million better off, and Wales would be £6 million better off. At the same time, however, the Treasury would lose £5 million in revenue that could otherwise be spent at the government's discretion, or used to reduce taxation. If the question were ever presented to Mrs Thatcher in this way – the economic benefit of Wales versus tax-cuts for the very rich – it wouldn't take many nanoseconds to work out the likely response! This is a decision a Tory government would have very little difficulty in making.

As a matter of historical record it was Plaid Cymru, through Ieuan Wyn Jones, that first raised the issue of Objective 1 in Westminster. There is an oft-repeated spin by Labour Party activists that Plaid Cymru had always insisted it was impossible to win Objective 1 but this is the reverse of the truth. Plaid Cymru always recognised that the change in boundaries was achievable, and that such a change would automatically lead to Objective 1 status for most of Wales. However, following meetings with the European Commission in 1997, Plaid Cymru leaders did express serious concern that unless Whitehall showed more urgency in pressing the issue the opportunity would be lost. This is the only basis of the claim that "Plaid Cymru said we would never win it".

To the credit of Ron Davies, then Secretary of State, the matter eventually got to the top of the government agenda. The revised boundaries were accepted by Eurostat so that the new

NUTS 2 region of West Wales and the Valleys, covering two-thirds of the population of Wales, had an average GDP of only 72.5 per cent the EU average and so became eligible for £1.2 billion of European Structural Funds.

Some critics outside Wales complained that the new boundaries were totally artificial and devised solely to win Objective 1 funding. In contrast, I would argue that the new NUTS 2 region of West Wales and the Valleys, including as it does the whole of Y Fro Gymraeg and Welsh Wales, reflects a genuine identity, one with a firm historical basis. It is difficult to define firm boundaries in medieval Wales but if we take the year 1200 AD and combine the total area controlled by the House of Gwynedd in the north and by the sons of Lord Rhys and his loyal supporters in the south, the geographical area under Welsh control in that year was very close to the present NUTS 2 region of West Wales and the Valleys. For example, the three castles traditionally associated with my ancestor Ifor Bach mark the exact boundary of the Objective 1 region south of Caerffili.[6]

It is equally significant that the 11 counties that voted 'Yes' in the devolution referendum are all included in West Wales and the Valleys, confirming that the boundary between Y Fro Gymraeg and Welsh Wales on the one hand, and British Wales on the other, is a boundary defined by prosperity. So this is a genuine boundary, but a boundary we should aim to eliminate as soon as possible to ensure that prosperity is spread to every part of Wales, thereby establishing a real unity in the country. This must be an over-riding aim of the Assembly Government's economic strategy.

But before we define the future agenda, it is instructive to consider how we arrived at the present situation where over the centuries, despite the lack of a separate Welsh government and full national status, despite the divisions within Wales (real or imagined), despite the very poor communications between different parts of Wales, and despite the economic setbacks, *er gwaethaf pawb a phopeth*, a strong sense of Welsh nationality has survived.

Chapter 4

THE SURVIVAL OF WALES

The theme of this essay is to compare the competing forces that have operated throughout the history of Wales, some creating division, others reinforcing unity. The balance between the two has been – and still is – very close. The result of the 1999 referendum was a remarkably apposite symbol of our whole history. The unifying forces have protected the concept of Wales as a separate nation through many centuries, but the divisive forces have always prevented Wales reaching its full potential.

I would like to outline very briefly how this balance has been maintained in many different aspects of our life and how – at last – with the creation of the National Assembly we might tip the balance significantly in favour of unity. Let us start with the geography of Wales. To what extent has geography determined the essential features of Welshness? This is a theme developed by many scholars, including the distinguished Welsh geographers E.G.Bowen and Estyn Evans.

In the first place, Wales is where the hills begin. Draw the 200 metre contour on a map of England and Wales south of the Wirral and you have drawn a close approximation to the boundaries of Wales. If you travel westward along the A40, the A465 or the A438 then Wales begins with the Black Mountains; and on the A44 it begins with Hergest Ridge. On the A489 the England-Wales boundary coincides with the Kerry Hills, and on the A458 with Long Mountain and Criggion. Along the A5 the Berwyns signal entry into Wales. Further north, the official boundary of Wales does extend to the low-lying area east of the Clwydian range and into Maelor Saesneg, a direct result of the territorial expansion of Gwynedd in the 12th century. However, only along the A48/ M4 can you penetrate far into Wales without actually entering the hills, and even on this road the Gwent hills appear a short distance to the north soon after the visitor crosses the Severn Bridge. Stand on Pen y Gadair Fawr in the Black Mountains, near the Welsh-English border, and you are at the highest point on the 51.95°N circle of latitude between Saskatoon and Novosibirsk.

These hills formed ideal territory for defensive warfare, allowing the indigenous population to counter invasion by conventional armies. This is where Caratacus retreated to continue his resistance to the Romans. Indeed, the influence of the Romans in Wales was always limited, which is why a Celtic language survived within the Roman Empire. Offa built his Dyke near the eastern boundary of the Welsh hills, setting a prudent limit to his territorial ambitions. The same geography prevented the Normans overwhelming Wales in the immediate aftermath of their conquest of England. One of their most serious defeats was at Ystrad Mynach, a battle celebrated by Walter Scott.

The castles of the Welsh princes, like Castell y Bere or Dolwyddelan, were castles of defence deep in the mountains. It is no coincidence that one of the first acknowledged guerrilla leaders in history was Owain Glyndwr, and his first major victory was at Hyddgen, near Pumlumon. (Che Guevarra was inspired by Owain Glyndwr and it is claimed that Fidel Castro keeps a book on Glyndwr on the shelves in his study).

The same hills created isolated communities, and in such communities families could continue undisturbed for centuries, preserving old customs and practices. My mother's mother came from Cwm Rhymni, growing up in Bargoed long before the coal industry arrived. We can trace that branch of the family, generation by generation, via the Lewises of Gilfach Fargoed and the Lewises of the Van in Caerffili, back to Llewelyn Bren, Ifor Bach, Iestyn ap Gwrgan and – possibly – Gwaethfoed. At this stage, in the 10th century, firm historical evidence fades into fantasy so on this occasion I won't follow the trail even further to Coel Hen or Macsen Wledig (though I sometimes do so to impress Americans!) I therefore feel a strong affinity with the squire of Cwmbychan, Evan Llwyd, who according to Thomas Pennant could trace his ancestors back for nineteen generations to 1100. There are few parts of Europe where such family stability over many centuries would be possible.

However, the same hills that defined and defended isolated and unchanging communities also posed a natural barrier to the integration of that common experience into a sense of nationhood. And here lies a paradox. It was this geography that made Wales difficult to conquer and helped preserve many of our national characteristics, including the language. Yet the same feature inhibited the development of national unity. In the south an elevated plateau is divided by the steep valleys of the Devonian trend with rivers like the Llwyd, Ebwy, Sirhywi, Rhymni, Taf, Ogwr and Tawe running north-south and impeding easy west-east travel, except along the coastal plain. In the north the Caledonian trend ran through ancient mountains from south-west to north-east. This provides an opening into Wales along the Dyfrdwy and the Bala cleft but still makes a nightmare of the journey along the A470 from south-east to north-west.[7]

So geological structure did made communication difficult, and not only did it cut off north from south: it also divided neighbouring communities, I grew up in Bargoed exactly six kilometres from Bedlinog, yet I did not set eyes on Bedlinog until I first fought an election in a constituency that included the village. For me it was dedicated politics that eliminated the barrier between Bargoed and Bedlinog.

Actually, it was also a final trace of Norman influence that in 1964 Bedlinog was still politically linked with Bargoed. In flat Normandy the obvious definition of a territorial boundary was always a river, so after the Plantagenet conquest of Wales most major boundaries followed rivers. As a result Bargoed was in the same constituency as Bedlinog but in a different constituency, a different county, and some used to say a different country from Aberbargoed, just across the river. Of course, in a territory dominated by steep valleys it is the watershed that should normally mark a boundary, but it was only following local government reorganisation in 1974 that this obvious fact was recognised in the redrawn boundaries of Wales. It was, of course, in the same re-organisation that for the first time the county of Gwent was legally confirmed as unequivocally part of Wales.

Chapter 5

STRENGTH IN DISUNITY

The history of the Norman Conquest leads to a second paradox, as striking as the paradox of geography. One comment by Giraldus Cambrensis in his memorable description of Wales is often quoted: "If Wales had a single leader, and he a good one, she would never be conquered. Inseparable she would be insuperable". In school, what little Welsh history I was taught repeated the same mantra: "Wales was defeated by the English because they were united under a single king whereas Wales was divided among quarrelling princes".

It was many years later, as a naïve scientist dabbling in history, that from the same received facts I came to a very different interpretation. In the first place, of course, Wales was never conquered by the English, but by the Norman Plantagenets. And whereas the conquest of England was effectively complete after one day it took a further 216 years to conquer Wales. And the reason? A single king ruled England, so when he was killed in Hastings the war was won. Wales was ruled by many princes so that, like a multi-limbed hydra, when one was defeated another would mount a surprise attack. As Harri Webb once pointed out to me, Llywelyn, Ein Llyw Olaf, Llywelyn the Last, was also Llywelyn the First because he was the first prince to exercise – if only for a fleeting moment – a supremacy over an area which covered almost the whole of modern Wales. That was why with his death in Cilmeri resistance crumbled. It is significant that according to one version of his death he was travelling in a small company in order to cover the distance from south to north as quickly as possible, and hence he was vulnerable to attack by a relatively small Norman force. It is equally significant that had he not quarrelled with his brother in time-honoured fashion, Dafydd might have perished with him in Cilmeri and all resistance collapse immediately. As it happened Dafydd carried on the fight for another year. So my paradox, counter to the assertion by Giraldus, is that in diversity – call it disunity if you will – lies our strength. Our national history has been poised between the two.

So let us now consider all those other aspects of our national life where there has been this continuing and miraculous balance between the forces that divide us and tie us more closely to England and those that bind us together as a nation.

Chapter 6

LAND OF THE BOOK

As a scientist I hate repeating orthodox, received opinion but in considering the social history of Wals I must start with religion as it has been so important. Perhaps the first expression of nationhood representing the whole peninsular of modern Wales was the convocation of bishops that met in 602 before going forth to greet Augustine on the banks of the Severn. It is claimed that this meeting took place in Llangoed, and if so Llangoed Hall can be regarded as the site of the first National Assembly. We all know what subsequently happened: Augustine neglected to greet the Welsh bishops with sufficient respect, and full unity with the Catholic Church was delayed for 166 years. Historians often explain the continuing disagreement in terms of the date of Easter and the shape of the tonsure. I feel it is more likely that behind these declared conflicts the true motivation for keeping the Welsh church separate was to preserve the status of married clergy.

Later on Giraldus Cambrensis made valiant and repeated attempts to re-establish the religious identity of Wales, but failed. Nevertheless, by the time of the Tudors Wales was devoutly Catholic and it was only through an over-riding loyalty to the Tudors as a dynasty that Wales reluctantly accepted the reformation. It was in this context that Elizabeth authorised the translation of the Bible into Welsh. This authorisation was permissive and not imperative, and certainly included no built-in guarantee that the translation would actually occur. Indeed it is possible that very little would have happened were it not for the single-minded dedication of Bishop Morgan.

It is said that Elizabeth's declared intention was to facilitate the opportunity of monoglot Welsh people to learn English by comparing the English and Welsh versions of the Bible, lying side by side in every parish church. (Oh, if only the learning of a language was as easy at that!) The real policy of the Tudors was, of course, to integrate Wales more completely within a unified English state rather than encourage the separate identity of Wales, and part of that policy was to bind Wales into the protestant Church of England.

To quote the usual cliché, the rest was history – and in this case it has often been presented as the main theme of our history between the sixteenth and nineteenth centuries. The sequence from Bishop Morgan's translation to Griffith Jones's circulating schools, Mary Jones and her bible, the Methodist Revival and eventually the confession of faith of a separate Calvinist connection, in a building that is now a high-street store, was the improbable chain of events that contributed immeasurably to the unity of Wales.

In assessing the miracle of Wales's survival as a nation it is worth considering all the alternatives that might have happened. As in Ireland, it may have been the old allegiance to Rome that retained the loyalty of Wales. Or, instead, all Wales might have been fired with enthusiasm for the first nonconforming evangelists, including the early Puritans such as William Wroth and Vavasor Powell, or the Quakers under William Penn, or the Unitarians with Richard Price from Llangeinor strongly influenced by Priestley, Bayes and Franklin: all of these causes were essentially English-centred.

When Methodism came it could have similarly been dominated by the charismatic influence of John Wesley, and of the four great exhorters Howel Harris at least had very strong links with England. Given, in addition, the continuing difficulties of communication between different parts of Wales, and the far easier access across the border to the market towns of England, the factors militating against the growth of independent Welsh churches were very strong. This may indeed explain the sudden disappearance of the Welsh language in Radnorshire, but the same could so easily have happened throughout Wales.

However, it is said that some of the leaders of the Methodist revival, such as William Williams Pantycelyn and Howel Harris, spent a large part of their waking hours in the saddle, travelling from village to village throughout Wales, and this single-minded determination broke down the barriers of distance. This crucial stage in the development of national consciousness in Wales was the direct result of the dedication of a small number of exceptional people, a theme that occurs again and again in our story.

The establishment of separate Welsh churches, bitter rivals though they often were, created a religious entity in Wales. My great aunt living under Mynydd Du in Carmarthenshire, kept photographs of Hoelion Wyth Undeb yr Annibynwyr from all parts of Wales. My great uncle Gwilym Thomas from Bargoed became a Minister, first in Arthog and then in Penmaenmawr. His brother started as a Minister in Beaufort, near Tredegar, but ended his career in the Llŷn. Another great uncle from Gwynfe in Carmarthenshire became a Minister in Corris.

It must, of course, be realised that by the end of the nineteenth century, for the first time ever, the network of railways serving almost every town in Wales made travel from one part of Wales to another relatively straightforward. Indeed it has been argued that the level of communication within Wales, and the consequent sense of national unity, reached a peak just before the First World War. As late as the 1940s, before Lord Beeching struck, I remember travelling by rail from Bargoed to Bangor via Pontypool, to Llandovery via Brecon and Builth, and to Neath via Aberdare.

The growth of non-conformity obviously made a huge positive contribution to our sense of national unity but it also contributed in an indirect, more negative way. The negative achievement was the disestablishment of the Anglican Church and the setting up of the Church in Wales, succeeding where Giraldus had failed. It is ironic that it is in this largely post-Christian age that for the first time a Welsh-speaking Welshman, Dr Rowan Williams, has become leader of the Anglican Church. A hundred years ago this could have been as anglicising an influence as Lloyd George becoming prime minister.

Chapter 7

RÔLE OF GOVERNMENT

While religion was preserving the unity of Wales and defying the barriers of geography, the irreversible growth of government was for many centuries a factor tying Wales more and more to England, and doing nothing – deliberately or otherwise – to develop a sense of separate Welsh nationhood.

After the Act of Union the only significant part of Government that treated Wales differently from England was the Council of Wales and the Marches in Ludlow and the organisation of the judiciary. The establishment of the Court of Great Sessions was a straightforward response to the sparse population and difficult communications within Wales. It was, of course, this purely pragmatic recognition of the distinctive geography of Wales that led to the intermittent claim that Monmouthshire, part of the Oxford circuit, was English. Actually by the same definition Cheshire would have been Welsh, but of course the Act of Union was intended to eliminate any idea of Wales as a separate nation.

In the course of time even these last vestiges of distinctiveness were eliminated. The Council of Wales and the Marches was abolished in 1688, following a period of greatly reduced importance. The Court of Great Sessions carried on for over a century longer but it finally came to an end in 1830 and with it went the last vestige of constitutional distinctiveness. Thereafter for over a century the agencies of Government largely disregarded Wales as a separate entity.

Thus, until the 1960s there were very few pieces of specifically Welsh legislation, though it must be admitted that those few were very significant. They included the Aberdare Act that established the University of Wales together with a network of grammar schools; Sunday Closing of Pubs in Wales and Monmouthshire; the Disestablishment of the Anglican Church in Wales; and the Welsh Courts Act. There were also two sections of Government administration that were devolved to Wales – the Board of Health and the Education Department. In parallel we must remember the founding of a National Library and a National Museum, two institutions that acquired a special importance in a nation devoid of the normal apparatus of nationhood. However, when all these are compared with the increasing volume of legislation and the total of Government administration they add up to very little.

The disregard of Wales as a separate nation was blatantly demonstrated by the Attlee government in 1945-51. There was never any possibility that this government would honour the long-standing Labour Party commitment to self-government for Wales. Under the influence of the Webbs Labour had become a state-centralist party and this was the theoretical justification for leaders of the party, like Bevan and Morrison, to oppose any measure of devolution. However, the cynic might agree that whatever theoretical arguments were advanced, the crucial point was the way in which the survival of the Labour Party in Westminster after 1935 depended so heavily on Welsh MPs. This was the case that convinced party managers to oppose any recognition of Wales that might ultimately lead to separatism.

For the same reason the Attlee government refused to appoint a Secretary of State for Wales, although this had been promised in the election manifestoes of several Labour MPs who pressed hard for such an appointment in 1946. The Attlee administration even failed to recognise Wales as a territorial unit. Between Government departments and nationalised industries this government set up a large number of public bodies with a regional structure. However, it seems that no two of them had the same regional boundaries. Within the National Coal Board the coalfield in south Wales was linked with Somerset and the Forest of Dean, and that in the north with Lancashire. For electricity generation Wales was linked with England, while Scotland was treated as a separate region. Meanwhile, for electricity distribution the South Wales Electricity Bord was set up to cover the south, and the north was linked with Merseyside in MANWEB, despite the strong objections of Jim Griffiths in Cabinet. Railway regions followed boundaries radiating outwards from London with most of Wales in the Western Region. Railways in the north belonged to the London Midland Region despite being remote from London and certainly not part of the English Midlands. Within the organisation of the Post Office Wales was linked with the Marches. Only for gas was Wales recognised as a natural unit.

Later Labour governments displayed a similar disregard for Wales as a logical unit. In the regional structure of the renationalised steel industry Wales was joined with Scotland. The nationalised water industry established Welsh Water covering most of Wales – except for those parts of mid-Wales that were allocated to Severn-Trent. These developments not only ignored the national identity of Wales, they even failed to establish common boundaries 'coterminosity' in England. This oversight surely lies at the root of the subsequent failure to develop a genuine regional consciousness in England. Hence the move towards coterminosity in the geographic boundaries of government bodies in Wales, with the same four regions now accepted by the WDA, WTB, Elwa and the Assembly Regional Committees, is one of the less-recognised achievements of the National Assembly. It is ironic that the main culprit that is now out of step is the Assembly itself, with five regions for the regional list election.

There was only one concession to Welsh sentiment in Westminster during the 1945-51 government This was the establishment in 1948 of a Council for Wales and Monmouthshire to advise the government on Welsh affairs. It was made up of 27 appointed members, initially under the chair of Huw T. Edwards, a trade-union leader from the north. It was unelected, had no powers, and met *in camera* with no report of its meetings published in the public domain. The best one-sentence summary of the Council could be copied from the judgement of the New Statesman when – in a similar spirit – the Welsh Grand Committee was set up in 1960 as a feeble Westminster response to the Parliament for Wales campaign: "It exists because Wales is a nation; it is not given any power in case Wales behaves as a nation". Nowadays some of us are tempted to say the same about the National Assembly.

Chapter 8

THE WELSH ECONOMY

There was one exception to the dismissal of Wales as a territorial unit in government structures. The Ministry of Reconstruction did recognise Wales as an Economic Planning Region. The 1944 Economic Plan, drawn up by the Welsh Reconstruction Advisory Council, was a significant landmark in regional economic planning. It is a sad reflection on our history that this was motivated by severe economic deprivation in the whole of Wales. By the 1920s the economy of both the north and the south had developed an overwhelming dependence on coal and steel, with over 40 per cent of the adult male population in Wales, a total of 373,000 men, employed either in Mining and Quarrying (mainly coal) or in Metal Manufacture (mainly iron and steel). Hence, the depression of the 1930s devastated Wales. It was the uniformity of deprivation in every part of Wales, north and south, that created an empirical reason for treating Wales as a unit within the 1944 Ministry of Reconstruction.

It is worthwhile recalling that the 1944 plan recognised the importance of good communications within Wales, and gave 'high priority' to a north-south road from Holyhead to Cardiff. As this project had already been under serious discussion since 1931 they recommended that the Government should plan the exact route 'without delay' and that such a road should be included in any post-war schedule of major public works, supported by a 100 per cent Exchequer grant. Despite this 'priority' it was almost 50 years before the dual carriageway to Merthyr was built, and the improvements to the A470 further north are still not complete, with the next major programme scheduled to start in 2008. With luck the road will be finished within 85 years of the first serious consideration[8]. Meanwhile the M4 and the A55 dual carriageways running west-east have been completed.

Later on, in 1958 a Development Corporation for Wales, forerunner of the WDA, was set up with Sir Miles Thomas as its Chairman. About the same time there was a very significant event in university circles, the publication of the Nevin reports on *The Social Accounts of the Welsh Economy*. This was the very first attempt to compare total government expenditure in Wales with the total revenue raised by the government from Wales. Nevin concluded that the accounts were more-or-less in balance. This destroyed a long-held assumption that Wales was subsidised by England. A copy of the first report, a fading, cyclostyled pamphlet of 48 pages from 1955, is one of my prized possessions and a truly historic document. Printed editions of the report followed in 1956 and 1957. These reports played an important rôle in persuading me to join Plaid Cymru in 1961.

The use of the term 'the Welsh economy', albeit in harmless academic circles, caused great astonishment. An annual dinner for businessmen in Swansea was addressed by Fred Cartwright, the head of the Steel Company of Wales. He dismissed the very idea of a separate Welsh economy and to illustrate the point he claimed that he had looked up the Welsh word for 'entrepreneur' in an English-Welsh dictionary and discovered that no such word existed. When asked what the English word was for 'entrepreneur' his total bewilderment was very illustrative.[9] Even more significant than the social accounts was Nevin's 1966 publication *The Structure of the Welsh Economy*. This included a full input-output matrix of the different elements in the Welsh economy, and on the basis of a continuing decline in the coal industry Nevin predicted a loss of 43,000 in the total number of jobs in Wales between 1964 and 1970. This conclusion was dismissed by Labour as a 'product of the ivory tower' and the government preferred the more optimistic predictions of Nevin's greatest academic rival in Wales, Brinley Thomas. The number of jobs actually fell by 48,000, very close to Nevin's prediction. However, he learned the hard way that in politics you might sometimes be forgiven for being wrong but you are never, ever forgiven for being right. From then on Nevin was totally marginalised by the government.

When we recall that Nevin helped to lay the foundations of the Irish economic miracle we see what a loss this was to Wales. A prophet is not without honour save in his own country ... Nevertheless, *The Structure of the Welsh Economy* was the basis for *An Economic Plan for Wales* published by Dafydd Wigley and myself in 1970, and Nevin gave us considerable help in this work. To be fair to his memory, what Nevin intended to show – for he was no nationalist – is that in economic planning the inter-reaction of all elements in the economy must be considered on a regional basis, and he chose Wales as his laboratory. His work illustrated the poverty of thinking of those centralists in the Attlee government who assumed that all planning should be done in Whitehall and that all inter-sector co-ordination should only take place at that level.

Even when politicians conceded the principle of regional planning the idea of an economic plan for Wales was still strongly opposed by other academics in the 1960s. Instead they wanted to replace Wales as an economic planning region with a North Wales and Merseyside region dominated by Liverpool, and a Severnside Region linking south Wales and the west of England with Bristol as the obvious capital.

It has always intrigued me whether proposals such as these were neutral academic exercises by technocrats who simply failed to recognise the importance of nationhood, or even its existence in the case of Wales, or whether there was a motivation – perhaps subconscious – to create structures that actively blocked any recognition of Welsh nationhood. The same question arose in considering the decisions of the Attlee government. Was the total absence of coterminosity in the regional structures of government agencies and nationalised industries a consequence of uncoordinated government, where each Minister acted independently in establishing a command chain centred on Whitehall with whatever ad-hoc regional structure seemed suitable? Or was it a deliberate attempt to inhibit regionalism and consolidate the power of the centre? There is no doubt that some Welsh politicians like Ness Edwards and Aneurin Bevan were committed centralists and showed a marked hostility to any institutional recognition of Welsh nationhood.

It is a measure of the changing situation that today, with the territorial integrity of Wales fully established since 1974 and the National Assembly in place, some of us in Plaid Cymru feel free to propose a Severnside International Airport serving Wales, the west of England and the English Midlands. This was an idea that we rejected as an abomination in the 1960s.

Chapter 9

DEVOLUTION

Given the dominance of Labour in Wales, and the prominence that the early Labour Party had given to the aim of Welsh Home Rule, it is puzzling that the first real move to recognise the existence of Wales at the highest levels of government occurred under Churchill. After returning to office in 1951 he established the strange hybrid of Home Secretary and Minister for Welsh Affairs, a post held first by Sir David Maxwell-Fyfe – 'Dai Bananas' as he was widely called – and later by Gwilym Lloyd-George and Henry Brooke. This position was subsequently enhanced by the additional appointment of Lord Brecon as a Minister of State for Wales. In the meantime (1955) Cardiff had been designated as capital of Wales.

The formal designation of a 'Welsh Office' also occurred under the Tories, during the period when Macmillan was Prime Minister. However, the real turning point was undoubtedly the appointment of Jim Griffiths as Secretary of State in 1964. There is a story of how Aneurin Bevan, the committed centralist, had initially opposed the creation of a Secretary of State but just before his death a mellow, less controversial Bevan was overheard in one of the corridors of Westminster saying to Jim Griffiths "Well, if you want it so much you had better have it!"[10]

From then on there has been a logical progression. It is to the credit of Jim Griffiths, as Charter Secretary of State, and Harold Finch, his Minister of State, that they insisted on obtaining for the Welsh Office far more powers than originally intended. Further powers were then added during the course of the 1964-70 Wilson government. Once the powers of the Welsh Office had increased the range of responsibilities became too much for a Secretary of State and a Minister. More and more functions were delegated to Quangos, and this stimulated the question of accountability, an issue especially controversial under a Conservative administration that did not have, and has never had, a democratic mandate from Wales. Hence the next logical step was inevitably an elected body. With the establishment of the National Assembly a decisive move to consolidate the territorial integrity of Wales was taken. This can be described either as the inevitability of gradualism or alternatively as a slippery slope: the description chosen depends on political stance.

One question that needs to be resolved is why the disjointed geographic functionalism of the Attlee administration was replaced by a gradual recognition of the identity of Wales. Was it the subtle pressure of patriots like Jim Griffiths, Cledwyn Hughes, Goronwy Roberts, Megan Lloyd-George and S.O.Davies in the Labour Party – or even Wyn Roberts in the Tory Party? Was it driven by a sense of guilt at a time when the countries of the old British Empire were, one-by-one, winning their independence? Was it a simple political recognition of the relative success of the Parliament for Wales campaign in the 1950s, and the results of the subsequent General Election in 1959, where Plaid Cymru fought 20 seats and won 80,000 votes? Or was it a response to the beginning of a more militant nationalism? Gwynfor Evans claims that the very first invitation he had to a meeting with a government minister (Keith Joseph) followed shortly after an explosion at a reservoir site.

Whatever the different factors that built up a case for devolution, it is undoubtedly true that in the end the demand for a recognition of national identity became stronger than the opposition. In other words more people actively wanted Wales to be a nation than those who actively opposed the idea. As with the growth of nonconformity this was the result of the dedication of a small number of exceptional people. Needless to say, the majority of people were largely unaware of the debate.

Chapter 10

THE POLITICAL PARTIES AND
THE UNITY OF WALES

It is the attitudes of political parties and their individual members that eventually determine the attitude of government. Who was the first MP in Westminster who in some way or other felt a special responsibility for the whole of Wales? Probably it was Henry Richard, the 'Member for Wales'. The best account of this period comes in Kenneth Morgan's *Wales in British Politics*, which describes the emergence of Cymru Fydd, the first true political organisation aiming to represent the whole of Wales.

Why should such an organisation appear at this time? It clearly followed the example of other nationalist movements throughout Europe, especially in Ireland and Italy. The development of a railway system – albeit centred on London – made possible a degree of interaction between different parts of Wales never seen before. The extension of the electoral franchise led to the joint triumph of the chapels and the working class in the 1868 election. But it was only a partial triumph. The barriers of distance were still a factor when in 1896 Lloyd George travelled from Caernarfon to Newport in an attempt to persuade the South Wales Liberal Federation to join Cymru Fydd. The meeting was a total disaster. Lloyd George was attempting to overcome the physical and psychological barriers between north and south and he failed. This marked the end of Lloyd George as nationalist and a few years later he re-invented himself as imperial leader.

Part of the problem in 1896 must surely have been the lack of close personal contact in a country with poor communications. Despite the rail network, until the era of mass car ownership this would remain a problem in any attempt to organise a political movement, or any other movement, on an all-Wales basis. Plaid Cymru itself was an amalgamation of two movements – one based in Penarth and one in Caernarfon. It is neatly symbolic that D.J. Williams failed to attend the inaugural meeting of the new, combined party in Pwllheli in 1925 because of a missed train connection. It is also significant that for many years – indeed from the first occasion in 1926 until the 1960s – Plaid Cymru's annual Summer School and Conference were always held on the weekend before the Eisteddfod, in a nearby venue. It was felt that if members had to make a long and difficult journey, it was just as well to do it once and make the most of it. This, of course, is the reason why the Eisteddfod itself still alternates from north to south, hence giving the maximum opportunity for ordinary people to attend at least one year in two, a sensible principle that had once justified the migration of the Court of Great Sessions.

As a reward for the effort of attending Plaid Cymru conferences after 1961 I shared with many other young people the pleasure of discovering a new part of Wales every year. Nevertheless it was Llandrindod and Aberystwyth which benefited most from the emergence of all-Wales political movements. As the rival queens of mid-Wales, they enjoyed the privilege of being equally distant from everywhere, and equally inconvenient for everyone.

Eventually, despite the failure of Lloyd George in 1896, the Liberals formed a Welsh Liberal Party, with a clear commitment to a full parliament for Wales within a federal UK constitution. Unfortunately by the time this commitment was fully established in the 1960s, the Liberals had ceased to be a major political force, either in Wales or in the UK.

In the early days, the Labour Party expressed a similar commitment to 'Home Rule' for Wales. Unfortunately, by the time Labour achieved power the elements that stressed the importance of centralised state control had taken over and the commitment was initially forgotten. Only gradually did the party restore the recognition of Wales and introduce devolution into its policies. The setting up of a Welsh Regional Council of Labour in 1947, and the establishment of a Wales TUC in 1974 (to whose inaugural conference I had the privilege of being a delegate) were important steps. However, as the late Val Feld once explained to me, until 1999 Labour in Wales had been primarily an election-winning organisation and not a policy-making body. There is no doubt that the establishment of the National Assembly, and the rôle of Labour as the dominant partner in the Assembly Government, marks a significant change. Differences of policy are emerging between the New Labour Government in London and the Assembly Government in Cardiff. How wide these differences may grow within a single UK Labour Party is one of the key questions for the future.

In reviewing the contribution of political parties to the unity of Wales the real surprise has been the rôle of the Conservatives. As a declared Unionist party that has always officially opposed the devolution of power to Wales the Conservatives in government have actually contributed greatly to the processes that made devolution inevitable. I have already mentioned that it was Churchill who first appointed a Minister for Welsh Affairs and Macmillan who established a Welsh Office, albeit without a Secretary of State. Even more surprisingly, the 1979-1997 Conservative governments initiated several crucial changes. It was the Tories who allowed a separate National Curriculum for Wales and insisted that the Welsh language should be taught to all secondary-school pupils up to the age of 16. It was also a Conservative administration that accepted a Plaid Cymru amendment to the Education Act that established a separate Higher Education Funding Council for Wales. Even more surprising, in face of intense if geriatric opposition from the academic establishment, the Conservatives established a separate Countryside Council for Wales. All of these contributed substantially to a trend that must have helped the success of the 1997 referendum. Furthermore, when the referendum itself is considered there is a question that historians will debate for decades: why did the Tories do so little to support the 'No' campaign?

There is no doubt, however, that the most obvious contribution of the Tories to establishing the Assembly was negative. Francis Cornford, in *Microcosmographia Academica*, pointed out that the most effective – if dangerous – way of winning a debate is to put a very bad argument in favour of the opposite case.[11] There is no doubt that the experience of the Thatcher government, and especially the period when John Redwood was Secretary of State, contributed substantially to the change of heart in the Labour Party between 1979 and 1997. To see so much power in Wales in the hands of Quangos that included prominent Tories out of all proportion to the electoral strength of the Conservatives in Wales – or indeed their intellectual resources – was a blatant affront to democratic principles. Perhaps more tellingly, it also happened to damage Labour's traditional hegemony.

The Tory Party has always been part Unionist and part English Nationalist, without realising any contradiction. Just ask your typical English Tory what is the fundamental difference between 'England' and 'Britain'. However, the more perceptive Tories have always recognised that Wales doesn't really belong to their vision of Britain. After a truly disastrous performance for the Tories in a Welsh by-election I remember Iain MacLeod stoically commenting on a television programme: "The Welsh worship different Gods!" I am sure that the Tories have also calculated the effect on party balance in Westminster if the Welsh (and Scottish) MPs were withdrawn or reduced in number.

The most intriguing aspect of all this, however, is the increasing importance of those Conservatives who have a genuine and deep commitment to Wales. They are, of course, outnumbered by those Tories from Wales, like Geoffrey Howe, Michael Heseltine, Kenneth Baker and Michael Howard, who reached high office in government but achieved very little benefit for their country of origin. But it is intriguing to estimate the overall contribution that Wyn Roberts made during his period in the Welsh Office where he was often the only Minister with any real understanding of Wales.

It is always dangerous to attach too much long-term importance to a recent event, but I am convinced that the 2002 Annual Lecture of the Institute of Welsh Politics, given by Lord Griffiths of Fforestfach and dealing with the future of Conservatism in Wales, will have a noticeable impact at a time when the Conservative Party is in disarray. Here was one of Mrs Thatcher's closest advisers arguing that to have a future in Wales the Conservative Party must be seen as a Welsh party, not as a foreign party operating in Wales. From this he concluded that the Conservatives must, from now on, fully engage in the process of devolution. He linked this with an ideological commitment to subsidiarity, a principle that allows the greatest freedom of action to the individual and the community[12]. Here are the principles on which a Welsh Conservative Party could transform its position in Welsh political life. If this happens we will have, for the first time, a situation where every major political force in Wales has a genuine Welsh dimension.

One question will then remain to be answered: to what extent is the development of a full Welsh polity an inevitable historical trend and to what extent is it a direct response to the growth of Plaid Cymru? Within the Party of Wales there is a recurring debate as to whether an essential pre-requisite for self-government is that Plaid Cymru replaces the Labour Party as the mainstream, dominant party in Wales. Alternatively, is it possible for a single-minded and uncompromising Plaid Cymru to create the conditions whereby other parties deliver self-government, albeit step-by-step and with some reluctance. Progress over the past forty years, and especially the establishment of the National Assembly, point to the latter strategy.

Chapter 11

MEDIA

Closely linked to political life are the media. Consequently, the extent to which they serve the unity and identity of Wales must also be considered. Here the geographic problems of overland communication have dictated another important factor in the life of Wales – the circulation of daily newspapers. When the mass press emerged in the early twentieth century circulation was dictated to a large extent by railway timetables. One reason why Scotland retained its own independent press to such a degree was that in those days trains from London to Scotland took too long for London papers to reach Scotland in time for early morning delivery. Newspapers like the *Scotsman* and the *Glasgow Herald* could succeed without serious competition from the equivalent London press. However, newspapers from London could arrive in Cardiff and the Valleys in time for the morning paper round, so a separate Welsh Press did not achieve the same total penetration – except in west Wales where the train from London arrived too late. As a result, until the 1960s the *Western Mail* had saturation sales in Ceredigion and much of Carmarthenshire and Pembrokeshire. The recent decline in overall *Western Mail* circulation is not only a matter of quality. Those faithful old customers in west Wales are dying off and the distribution of London dailies is now so rapid that their children can choose the popular tabloids.

It has been estimated that only about 15 per cent of newspapers bought in Wales are published in Wales; the comparable figure in Scotland is 85 per cent. This must surely be a major reason why national consciousness is stronger in Scotland than in Wales. Many London newspapers give very little in-depth coverage of news from Wales except in the sports pages. Someone who lives in Wales and only reads a London newspaper could be totally unaware of many aspects of Welsh political life. Some time ago, for instance, I consulted the published annual index of articles in *The Guardian* and found that over several years there was not a single reference to Plaid Cymru.

Originally it was the same problem of distribution that prevented the *Western Mail* gaining a mass readership in the north and become a truly national paper. Once the Liverpool *Daily Post* had won a foothold it proved impossible to replace it, despite several worthy campaigns to win new readers in the north. As a result, the absence of a serious and widely-read national newspaper in Wales is one of the huge gaps in the emergence of a full national life. As it happens, both the *Western Mail*, the *Daily Post* and the *Welsh Mirror* are owned by the same company, as are many of the weekly regional papers. Consequently Trinity-Mirror have a near monopoly of Welsh newspapers, a situation that would cause great concern if it occurred in any independent country of the same size as Wales, but is accepted without question as merely a local dominance within the United Kingdom.

One bright feature in the present state of newspapers readership in Wales is the plethora of *Papurau Bro*. These reinforce the very local sense of community that remains a core feature of our national identity, the diversity from which we must forge our unity. Here, yet again, we see the contribution that a small number of dedicated individuals can make in demonstrating that the massive forces of multinational capitalism can be effectively mitigated. May they long continue their work, work that often receives scant recognition.

The development of radio and television in Wales was also frustrated by geography, though there was a reasonably happy ending. The early BBC was under the dictatorial control of Lord Reith who had little time for the Welsh language and very little time for Wales. Reith claimed that the mountainous topology of the country made it impossible to provide

Wales with our own, separate radio service. As a result south Wales was joined with the West of England in a BBC region fancifully called the 'Kingdom of Arthur', a precursor of Severnside. A prominent member of my pantheon of Welsh heroes is Eddie Bowen, a radio scientist from Swansea. As a student he published a series of technical articles showing in detail how a separate service for Wales could indeed be provided, and hence demonstrating without fear of contradiction that Lord Reith was either an incompetent radio engineer or simply dishonest. According to the BBC archives the noble Lord was not well pleased, but at least he recognised that Bowen was technically right. Hence the Welsh Home Service was established, an institution that has played an immensely important rôle in reinforcing the unity of Wales, with I.B.Griffiths becoming as popular in the south as E. Eynon Evans in the North.[13]

It can be convincingly argued that the establishment of the Welsh Home Service was the most important single factor in preserving a sense of national unity at a time when in so many other fields the sense of a separate Welsh identity was weakening. It is significant and appropriate that BBC Wales has always put more emphasis on a high quality, all-Wales radio service in both languages than on a large number of local radio stations.

The problems of geography were repeated with the establishment of the television service. Because television requires far higher frequencies than radio, and signals at such frequencies tend to travel in straight lines, there were genuine problems in providing an all-Wales service. The mountains of Wales meant that many parts of the country were able to receive a signal from an English transmitter to the east or south long before there was an accessible station transmitting programmes produced in Wales. Before 1982 the problem was aggravated by the way in which Welsh-language programmes were broadcast as occasional opt-outs on both BBC1 and ITV1. Households where no-one spoke Welsh were tempted to point their TV aerials permanently towards an English transmitter, even though this meant that the 'local' news and sports programmes dealt with the west of England or Lancashire. The establishment of S4C not only provided a more complete television service in Welsh, stimulating an exciting growth in the film and animation industry, but it also gave BBC1 Wales, HTV and, later, BBC2 Wales the opportunity to win back audiences to channels that broadcast an increasing number of English-language programmes originating in Wales. Once again a crucial advance was the direct result of an intense campaign by a relatively small number of totally dedicated individuals, in this case the members of Cymdeithas yr Iaith, culminating in 1980 with Gwynfor Evans' threat to fast to the death if the Government continued to renege on its 1979 election promise to establish a Welsh-language television channel.

In theory, the technical problem in providing an all-Wales television service was more or less solved with the construction of a network of local uhf transmitters providing almost complete coverage, and the development of digital television where signal compression can pack up to ten channels in the bandwidth previously sufficient for only one. Here the paradox is that the universal availability of Welsh television throughout Wales coincides with the huge expansion of channel choice. So in Aberystwyth I can now receive 45 free-to-air channels from the local transmitter. The historic problem arising from the restriction to local communication has very suddenly been transformed into the opposite problem of saturation by global communication. In the process there is an inversion of the psychology of distance.

Chapter 12

WALES! WALES!

Sport is another important area of human activity where the forces uniting and dividing Wales have been in balance, and where once again the unifying forces have proved much stronger than one might have expected. Let me start with a question that has long puzzled me. As is well known, rugby was a product of English public schools and universities, with the original rules devised at a conference in Cambridge. In Wales the sport was initially confined to the south-east of the country, with the first prominent rugby teams, such as Newport, including a large number of English-born players. In these circumstances, why was it that from the beginning, and so unequivocally, Wales established a separate Rugby Union and set up a national team to compete with England, Scotland and Ireland? Soccer poses a similar anomaly. The problems of distance within Wales, combined with easy access to England, have militated against a really successful Welsh league, and our best teams and our best players have always competed in the English league. Many young people in Wales, including committed nationalists, regularly support the leading English teams. Yet from the start there has been a separate Welsh International Football team and after years in the doldrums recent successes have fully justified its existence.

This didn't happen in cricket where a successful Welsh team only emerged recently, after the establishment of the National Assembly. Yet the pattern established in cricket is the pattern we might have expected. Why, from the very beginning, did Wales achieve full national status in both codes of football, as well as in so many other sports, despite the strong countervailing arguments in favour of strong all-UK teams, such as the British Lions?

The answer is partly contained in that phrase 'from the very beginning'. Team sport was arguably England's greatest and most enduring contribution to world culture, but before their global expansion occurred most of these sports were only pursued within the UK. As a result, in the early days it was only possible to have an 'international' match if it took place between the four home countries. The existence of four teams offered many more young players the chance of playing internationally. The fact that the separate Rugby Unions and Football Associations of the four nations of the UK are much older than almost all corresponding bodies in other countries is the crushing response to the periodic complaint, especially from Latin America, that 'England is allowed to enter four teams in international competitions'. Perhaps the main justification for Wales in sport is that it is *not* England, another recurring theme in the development of Welsh unity.

Many committed patriots often decry 'football nationalists' but it is wrong to under-estimate the contribution that prowess in sport has made to the continuing sense of nationhood. Especially important have been those cases where Welsh sports men and women have become champions. In boxing we celebrate Freddie Welsh, Jim Driscoll, Jimmy Wilde, Tommy Farr, Howard Winstone, Johnny Owen and now Joe Calzaghe, champions all. This record is almost matched in snooker where Ray Reardon, Doug Mountjoy, Terry Griffiths and Mark Williams have all been world champions. In a long list of other sports, from horse-jumping to weight-lifting, from long-jumping to darts, from hurdling to cycling we treasure an impressive gallery of heroes.

As a cynical scientist I might be tempted to comment that there are so many different sports with so many different categories of competition that, on a purely statistical basis, a country of three million population might expect such a gallery of champions. But cynicism has no place when the young fan, coming from a community of multiple deprivation, enjoys a moment of sheer ecstasy as someone from Wales, and especially someone from his or her own Valley, wins a world championship. In those areas that have suffered decades of decline people have lost so much. They may have no hope of steady employment, they have been denied prosperity, their young people have had to leave home: Welshness is the one thing of value that no-one can take away. When Wales is on top their joy is in direct proportion.

How else can we explain the widespread sense of Welsh nationality, as recorded in the ONS Survey, among a population who, by-and-large, do not speak Welsh, do not read Welsh publications, do not watch many TV programmes produced in Wales, and may not even bother to vote in Assembly elections? Like an underground stream that suddenly appears on the surface, there is an enduring and fundamental sense of nationhood that cannot be ignored. I am old enough to remember when some organisers refused to play *Hen Wlad Fy Nhadau* before the kick-off in international matches played outside Wales. This had become a burning issue, and by happy chance I happened to be present at that Wales-France match in the old Cardiff Arms Park when – for the first time – the crowd heeded the slogan 'One Nation, One Anthem' and booed *God Save the Queen* with such unanimous and unmistakable enthusiasm that soon afterwards it was only played on occasions when it was appropriate, such as matches against England. Some of my friends, who were also at that match, afterwards confessed to a totally unexpected sense of liberation. Sometimes, in ways that we intellectuals totally fail to understand, there are loyalties to Wales among ordinary people that represent a huge, positive potential in Wales that so far we have largely failed to exploit.

Chapter 13

RÔLE OF THE ASSEMBLY

So what of the future? Despite all the disappointments and frustrations some of us feel with the National Assembly, it has recorded an impressive number of achievements in a short time. The appointment of a Children's Commissioner, a more objective way of allocating money to local authorities, free entry to museums, free bus travel for pensioners and learning grants for students are some of the recognised successes.

However, in my opinion one of the biggest achievement of all is the one least noticed outside the Assembly itself. For the first time ever we see the growth of an all-Wales civic society. The National Assembly has become the focus for all public and voluntary bodies depending on – or seeking – support from the Assembly. My diary was filled during the four years of the first term with meetings where such bodies – often in co-operation with other organisations working in related fields – gathered together on an all-Wales basis to present their case to AMs. This brought active members of such organisations to Cardiff from all over Wales, often for the first time. In turn, this is creating natural networks that didn't exist before, a process further encouraged by the need to form partnerships to access European Structural Funds.

A very significant part of the process is the increasing tendency for UK bodies to establish, often for the first time, a separate Welsh regional organisation, with a headquarters and secretariat in Cardiff. I am a member of the Institute of Physics. There used to be a Liverpool branch covering the north, a Birmingham branch covering mid-Wales, and a branch in south Wales. This was a perverse division that made no practical sense at all as almost all the schools in Wales follow the same physics syllabus under the WJEC, and all the physics departments are in the University of Wales where they co-operate in a single faculty. A physicist in Aberystwyth in the late twentieth century, whether a schoolteacher or a university lecturer, had far more in common with Cardiff than with Birmingham. The old divisions didn't even make geographic sense as Swansea and Bangor were much closer to Aberystwyth than Wolverhampton and Warwick.

It would be flattering to Wales to suggest that the original regional structure was a deliberate attempt to counter Welsh unity. The fact is that the existence of Wales simply didn't register and it was only on 1999 January 1st that the regional structure of the Institute of Physics was reconstituted to form an all-Wales branch. On the very same day the Institute of British Innkeepers made a similar change. There had been a Lake District and North Wales Region and a West Country and South Wales Region. These were replaced by an all-Wales Region. I used to discuss with the new Vice President of the Welsh Region of the IBI, who kept the pub opposite my office in Tredegar, whether Physics or Inn-Keeping was more important. What really mattered is that these two changes were part of a trend that has involved dozens if not hundreds of other organisations recognising Wales for the first time.

It would be useful if someone would compile a complete list, and in a world with a chronic shortage of PhD topics someone is sure to do so. Not all these new bodies will be successful from the start, and the way funds were withdrawn from the Children's Society in Wales is both illuminating and disturbing. Some organisations may only be making a token gesture. But many of the new bodies are already fully engaged with the work of the Assembly, contributing to policy formation, feeding ideas to Ministers, AMs and department officials. In the best cases these organisations are also making regular contact with their own members in all parts of Wales so that when they lobby the Assembly they can genuinely claim to be representing the whole country.

One encouraging aspect of this new, emerging civic society is that until 1999 most of its professional members would have automatically been part of British Wales. Through their contact with the Assembly and Assembly-Sponsored Public Bodies they see an opportunity to make a difference in Wales as a whole in a way that was much more difficult through the old Welsh Office and virtually impossible through Whitehall. Once they sense a genuine response to their contributions they begin to identify with the work of the Assembly. Is it too optimistic to assume that this process is already contributing to a significant closing of the gap between Y Fro Gymraeg, Welsh Wales and British Wales in support for devolution? Surveys by the Institute of Welsh Politics at the University of Wales Aberystwyth show that between 1997 and 2001 support for a full Parliament steadily increased, while the number opting for no elected body fell substantially (see Table 1).

Table 1

Constitutional preferences in Wales, 1997, 1999 and 2001 (%s)

Constitutional Preference	1997	1999	2001
Independence	14.1%	9.6%	12.3%
Parliament	19.6%	29.9%	38.8%
Assembly	26.8%	35.3%	25.5%
No elected body	39.5%	25.3%	24.0%

What was also significant was that by 2001 these views were held broadly consistently across the country. Table 2 shows these constitutional preferences at the time of the 2001 Westminster election when mapped on to the 'Three Wales Model'. The combined preference for independence, a Parliament with legislative power and the present Assembly was still highest in Y Fro Cymraeg, at 82.5%, but followed very closely by Welsh Wales with 81.6 per cent. Even in British Wales the level of support was only a short way behind at 73.1 per cent.[14] Civic society is leading to civic nationalism.

Table 2

Constitutional Preferences by the Three Welsh Regions, 2001 (%s)

	Independence	Parliament	Assembly	No elected body
Y Fro Gymraeg	16.0%	38.0%	24.1%	17.5%
Welsh Wales	13.4%	38.6%	24.5%	18.4%
British Wales	8.8%	35.6%	25.2%	26.9%

Chapter 14

BRIDGING THE WEALTH GAP

What more can be done? Once we recognise the forces that have kept us apart – even when we share common interests – we can remove as many obstacles as possible. To achieve national unity the highest priority must be to establish economic unity. The worst feature of the Wales inherited by the National Assembly in 1999 was the unacceptable gap in average family income between deprived communities, whether in the mining valleys, in old steel-towns or in remote rural districts, and the relatively prosperous cities and towns along the M4 and the A55. This is the result of low wages, a very low employment rate and high levels of sickness and disability in the old industrial areas. The greatest failure of the National Assembly Government is that after four years the evidence suggests that this gap is growing rather than diminishing and that so far Objective 1 funds have made little difference.

This points to a serious fault in the economic strategy of the Assembly Government: the lack of any regional strategy linked with regional job targets. If the long-term aim is to reduce the gap in average GDP between Wales and the rest of the UK the most urgent first step must surely be to increase the employment rate in all parts of Wales to the present UK average.

In setting such targets at a regional level we must first define the appropriate regions within Wales, recognising fully that within the unity of any mature nation there is a healthy variety of regional diversity. Make these regions too small and it is impossible to combine the provision of infrastructure, training and investment in a full, integrated economic policy. That is the problem with basing economic development (or, indeed, health policy) on the 22 county councils. Make the regions too large and the problems of seriously deprived communities can be disguised by the performance of the neighbouring prosperous communities. That is a serious problem at present with the four WDA regions. Nevertheless, in the interests of coterminosity the boundaries of the chosen regions should be consistent with the WDA regions, and, where possible, consistent with the official European NUTS 3 regions.

In my opinion there are seven natural sub-regions in Wales. The north should be divided into the western part eligible for Objective 1 (Anglesey, Gwynedd, Conwy and Denbighshire); and the more prosperous eastern part (Flintshire and Wrecsam). Mid Wales should remain undivided (Powys and Ceredigion). The west should be divided into Dyfed (Pembrokeshire and Carmarthenshire) and Swansea Bay (Swansea and Neath Port Talbot). Finally, the south east – like the north – should be divided into the part eligible for Objective 1 (the old mining valleys of Bridgend, Rhondda Cynon Taf, Merthyr, Caerffili, Blaenau Gwent and Torfaen); and the coastal strip (Vale of Glamorgan, Cardiff, Newport and Monmouthshire). Once the sub-regions are defined it is elementary mathematics to measure the scale of the challenge in each case by calculating the number of extra jobs required to raise the overall employment rate for the working-age population to the UK average.

This calculation immediately brings into prominence the very different needs of the different sub-regions. In Swansea Bay and the Valleys the shortfall in employment is so large that it requires an extra 60,000 jobs to meet the target. At the other end of the spectrum, the employment rate in the north-east and in mid-Wales is already close to the UK average. What is needed in these regions is a smaller number of high-quality and highly-paid jobs to encourage young, educated people to find progressive employment near their home. The jobs needed in the other three sub-regions fall somewhere

in between. Without calculated targets it is impossible to moni-
tor the success of the economic strategy in spreading prosperity more evenly across Wales and to decide how the strategy
should be amended to boost any sub-regions falling behind.

The counter argument deployed by the Assembly Government is that any targets should be for Wales as a whole, as it
is impossible to direct business to a less favourable location.
This argument falls on two grounds. In the first place, if it is
impossible to direct business to a location why have targets
for Wales as a whole? Surely the aim is not to attempt Stalinist
direction by the State but to work in partnership to provide
the correct infrastructure, financial support and training fa-
cilities to make each region naturally attractive to the target
sectors.

Secondly, the result of the government's laisser-faire strategy is to create two highly-congested regions in the north-
east and south-east, with an over-heated local economy, while
at the same time wasting social and human capital in the
remaining, deprived areas. If we are to remove the barriers
between different parts of Wales we cannot tolerate the huge
prosperity gap between Gurnos and Gellideg at one end of
the Taff Valley, and Lisvane and Rhiwbina at the other. And
the same applies if we are to maximise our overall economic
success.

In recent years, as part of the study into the long-term ef-
fects of Structural Funds, the European Union has introduced
an index to represent the divergence in the prosperity of different regions within each member state. It is a stark reminder
of the way in which regional policy has been dismantled in
the UK that among the 15 EU members the disparity in regional prosperity is highest in the UK with an disparity index of 33.9 per cent, higher even than in Germany with the
division between the East and the West (26.8 per cent), higher
even than in Italy with the historic division between its north
and south (27.6 per cent).

Years ago the Breton nationalist Yann Fouere reminded me
that an endemic problem with the 'submerged' nations of
Europe is that we always tend to copy our masters. It fits this

analysis that while the UK is the one member state of the EU with no pretence of a regional policy the present Assembly Government feels compelled to reject any effective regional policy for Wales. Yet if we are to consolidate the new-found unity of Wales it must be our highest priority to eliminate the huge and growing differences in prosperity between Y Fro Gymraeg and Welsh Wales on one hand and British Wales on the other. Otherwise this will be the geological fault-line undermining all our national plans.

Chapter 15

COMMUNICATIONS

Improved physical communication between different parts of Wales, especially between north and south, must also be a high priority. An early step by the Assembly was to subsidise a daily direct rail service from Cardiff to Holyhead and back. I have used it for meetings in Llandudno and it is comfortable and convenient. In the near future we are to have an all-Wales railway franchise. If only responsibility for railways became a fully devolved function by 2004 we would automatically receive an extra £200 million a year in the Barnett block, and this could go some way to re-establish a full railway network in Wales as the core of an integrated passenger transport system.

It is an instructive exercise to examine the criteria used by Lord Beeching and his successors in British Rail to justify closing individual railway lines. There is a substantial literature on the huge deficiencies in the accounting methodology, especially on the way in which the costs of signalling and line-maintenance were divided between freight and passenger traffic on each line. What is even more significant in the case of Wales is the incompetent way in which individual lines were closed without any real assessment of the knock-on effect on other lines and on the whole network.

The tragedy in Wales is that two relatively minor closures, the lines between Pwllheli and Caernarfon and between Aberystwyth and Carmarthen, destroyed the one remaining north-south link within Wales. At a stroke these closures prejudiced any chance of developing an all-Wales rail network. At the same time the closure of the Aberystwyth-Carmarthen line had an immediate effect on the traditional links between schools in the south and the University College in Aberystwyth, and in a short time the West Midlands of England became the main catchment area for recruiting students rather than the Valleys. I'm sure it would not require extensive research to confirm that the effect of the closure on the national unity of Wales did not feature in the smallest possible way in the calculations of British Rail, though allegedly it was the threat to eight Labour-held marginal constituencies that preserved the mid-Wales line.

Subsequently no serious attempt was made to preserve the routes of the lines that were closed. I have at home a set of maps from the county planning department covering the old Aberystwyth-Lampeter railway. The route has been compromised in many places but perhaps the most significant detail is the point on the line where someone, surely someone in the planning department, has added in handwriting "A bungalow seems to have appeared here".

It may never be economic to restore all the railway lines that contributed so significantly to the developing sense of Welsh nationhood in the golden Edwardian age. However, in 2002 I attended a symposium on public transport in Baden-Württemberg in Germany. The branch railway line to Bad Urach had recently been restored as part of an ambitious integrated bus-rail service. In terms of the geographical nature of the area served, this would be the equivalent of restoring the Barmouth-Rhiwabon line so we must not ignore the increasingly important rôle of railways in all parts of a modern economy, both rural and urban. The criteria for success are that the restored services must be fast, frequent, reliable and comfortable enough to attract a sufficient number of present-day car users to choose rail as the more attractive alternative. This requires an adequate initial investment: I hope this will be the case when passenger services are reopened on the Ebbw Vale to Cardiff line.

Whatever the future of rail we must also create a modern,

all-Wales road system or the old barriers will still inhibit the full development of Wales as a nation. In 1970 Dafydd Wigley and I published an *Economic Plan for Wales* with a proposed road network, including a figure-of-eight configuration linking the four corners of our country. By 2003 most of this network is actually complete, but there are a few significant gaps. I have already mentioned the priority recommended in 1944 for an arterial road from Holyhead to Cardiff. Over the intervening 59 years improvements have been made but the present A470 between Builth Wells and Newbridge and between Caersws and Betws-y-Coed is still disgracefully inadequate for our main National Highway. A third gap in our original plan, that I have frequently encountered while I was an AM, is the stretch between Aberystwyth and Haverfordwest. In contrast with the enormous sums that have been spent over the years in improving west-east road links, the cost of completing our 1970 proposals is a small price for consolidating national unity. It is helpful that all our AMs who live in the north and in mid-Wales, and all the officials from Assembly-Sponsored Public Bodies, County Councils and the new all-Wales Voluntary Bodies, who now have reason to travel to Cardiff on a regular basis, recognise the problem and are exerting considerable pressure for improvement in exactly the right places.

There is one final element of communication that with my background I feel is especially important. It is absolutely vital that information technology is used to establish easy data communication, including high-quality video links, between all parts of Wales. With the introduction of broadband communication this is a facility that should become as common as the telephone and could make a dramatic difference in the ease of contact across Wales. At a stroke the psychological and geographic barriers of distance can be discounted.

For example, one application of this technology will be the greater co-operation between all the higher education institutions in Wales. For 12 years the three physics departments of the University of Wales have used a video link for

fourth year and post-graduate teaching. Now that Cardiff is
secure as the one international-class university in Wales I
sense there is far less demand for it to break away from the
rest of the University of Wales, and far more readiness to
help strengthen the provision of higher education throughout the country. The opening of medical campuses at Swansea and – possibly – Bangor, under the auspices of the School
of Medicine in Cardiff, is a very good sign of how the psychology of distance is changing. The proper use of
broadband communications allows a degree of co-operation
that was previously impossible.

Broadband communication will also facilitate the
dispersion of all civil-service jobs throughout Wales. Once
high-speed data links between offices are matched by high-
quality video communication then it no longer matters where
the offices are located. There is no longer any reason why
thousands of officials should work in a single building,
especially when that building is as ugly as the Assembly
building in Cathays Park; no reason whatsoever why the
administrative heart of the nation should be concentrated at
a single centre of traffic congestion. The plans to move Welsh
civil service jobs to centres such as Colwyn Bay, Caernarfon,
Aberystwyth and Merthyr Tydfil show one way in which the
Assembly can act directly to spread prosperity to all parts of
Wales. Another example allows the text-translators in the
Assembly to work from home, wherever that may be in Wales.
Schemes like these would do a great deal to dispel the
impression that the Assembly only cares about Cardiff and
the M4 corridor.

But before these plans can be fully realised the
appropriate IT infrastructure must exist. In 1994, when Plaid
Cymru first published a policy for bringing broadband
communications to every town and village in Wales, the
prospects were favourable. Many of our main telephone
exchanges were already linked by an optic-fibre 'backbone'.
Wales was one of the major centres for the manufacture of
optic fibre, and boasted a cluster of opto-electronic
industries. It was realistic to imagine that with a suitable

combination of public and private sector investment the technology existed that could give Wales a world-lead in establishing broadband connectivity.

Nine years later and that early promise has been entirely squandered. Wales is now lagging seriously behind the rest of the industrialised world. A recent report by the OECD Working Party on Telecommunications and Information Services Policies entitled *The Development of Broadband Access in OECD Countries* lists the total broadband penetration per 100 inhabitants in June 2001. The UK lies in 22nd place, with only 0.28 broadband connections per 100 inhabitants. This figure should be compared with the average of 0.82 for the EU, 1.96 for the OECD as a whole, 4.52 for Sweden and 13.91 for South Korea. At the same time, according to the Connectivity Index Wales had fallen to the very bottom of the 12 economic regions of the UK. Instead of being near the top of the Premier League Wales is now at the bottom of the Third Division.

The reason is two-fold. In 1994 a privatised British Telecom had inherited an enviable reputation for technical expertise, based on the research laboratories in Martlesham. It had the capability to 'fibre up' the UK, and the process was already well advanced in Wales. However, the decision by the Conservative Government to prevent BT from delivering television programmes via land-line removed the main commercial incentive to press on with the broadband infrastructure. The programme suffered a further set-back when BT paid £16 billion to the government for the third generation mobile-phone licences, an investment unlikely ever to be recovered.

The faltering of the private sector was more than matched by the total indolence of the government, both at a UK level and in the Assembly. As a result, at the end of the Assembly's first four-year term, the Assembly Government had failed to produce a detailed and comprehensive strategy to use the combination of a fibre backbone plus the existing copper-wire links to the home to bring broadband to every town and village, while using the available wireless frequencies to cover rural areas too far from a telephone exchange to allow a Digital Subscriber Line (DSL).

Two stark facts spotlight the failure. In the Objective One Programme a total of £73 million was earmarked for IT Infrastructure. At the end of 2002, three years into Objective One, not a single penny had been allocated. The Assembly Government had totally failed to appreciate how rapidly Wales was falling behind in this crucial area. The second piece of evidence is an appalling re-run of history. Whereas optic fibre is the optimum channel to carry broadband to towns and villages, in the short-term only wireless transmission can serve the sparsely-populated rural areas. Wireless frequencies are a scarce commodity, and in choosing the frequency bands most suitable for a hilly country with high rainfall, like Wales, a balance has to be struck between the lower frequencies, where there is an absolute shortage of bandwidth, and the higher frequencies, where bandwidth is abundant but transmission can only occur along exact line-of-sight and the signal is badly affected by rain.

The government recently announced an auction of the 3.4 GHz band and in selecting the best combination of bandwidth and ease-of-propagation this is one of the most suitable frequency bands for Wales. The Welsh Advisory Committee on Telecommunications recommended that two licences be issued to Wales for this band, one'covering the Objective One region and the second the rest of Wales and part of the Marches.

Incredibly, however, when the 15 licence regions were announced by the Department of Trade and Industry in January 2003 the existence of Wales was entirely ignored. North Wales was included in a crescent-shaped region dominated by Yorkshire and North Lancashire. Mid-Wales was stitched on to a dough-nut-shaped region surrounding Birmingham and reaching as far as Lincolnshire. Most of the south was linked with the south-west of England in a recreation of Lord Reith's 'Kingdom of Arthur', apart from a cut-out region called Severnside, based on Bristol but including Cardiff.

The proposed boundaries make no sense whatsoever, technically or politically. The enemies of Wales at the heart of government are making a last ditch stand. A barrage of protests were directed at the Minister, but he refused to change the decision. This remains a salutary warning that the battle continues.

Chapter 16

REACHING OUR FULL POTENTIAL

Of course, as with the television channels, improved information connectivity establishes closer links within Wales while simultaneously providing links with everywhere else in the world. The Welsh psychology of distance will only be overcome, and the all-Wales dimension will only succeed, if people want these things to happen. This is perhaps the most important message of this paper. The forces of disunity have included powerful forces of geography, history and central government, and they are still active. The forces of unity have depended on the wishes of many ordinary people and the determination of some of their leaders.

But why? It is an existential question why throughout the ages the survival of Wales has been so important to individuals. As Dafydd Iwan sang, *Dim ond ffwl sydd yn gofyn pam fod eira yn wyn*. But when Anne Robinson asked 'What is Wales for' what is our answer?

For me the unique feature of Wales is the tradition of social justice. Wales has existed to provide the political leaders who invented the words 'socialism' and 'co-operative', who fought for a system of international justice, and who introduced old-age pensions, a free health service and a comprehensive national insurance system.

For others it is the survival of a separate language, one of the oldest in Europe, enshrining separate values against all adversity. A separate language is a bulwark against the homogeneous values of a globalised, market-driven economy. It was Jean-Paul Satre who wrote "To speak Breton is a revolutionary act because while there are still Breton people, there are only French masses". He could easily have written the same about Yr Iaith Gymraeg.

To yet others the answer is the deep, visceral love they have for a beautiful country with an intimate landscape of amazing variety, a landscape that imposes a deep sense of belonging. This creates a determination to preserve it against all threats, a determination felt as strongly by many who have come to Wales to live as by those of us who claim family roots a thousand years deep.

Combine the social, cultural and environmental drives and you produce a red-green movement of great power. Above all we share a conviction that Wales could be better, could serve its people better, could serve the world better. We sense that for all its achievements in the past the potential is even greater.

It is therefore reassuring that the forces maintaining Wales as a nation are at last winning ground and if the full potential of the National Assembly is realised the full potential of Wales as a nation will also be realised.

NOTES

1 Dai Smith, *A Question of History*, Seren, 1999.
2 The lecture was published as *My Impressions of Wales*, London, 1927.
3 See Dennis Balsom, 'The Three Wales Model' in John Osmond (Ed.) *The National Question Again*, Gomer, 1985.
4 John Osmond, *Divided We Fall: The Politics of Geography in Wales*, IWA, January 2003.
5 See John Osmond, *Divided We Fall*, for maps of these divisions, pages 8-9.
6 It is annoying to have to report that modern historians, with a disturbing passion for the truth, have concluded that two of these castles were build by the Normans as a defence *against* Ifor Bach. However, the boundary they define is not in dispute.
7 This is one of the few profound differences between north and south. The Caledonian trend, running from south-west to north-east along the Bala cleft or the Menai Strait links the north of Wales with similar features in the highlands of Scotland, such as the Caledonian canal, the fjords and mountains of Norway, and – so it is claimed – the Appalachian mountains in West Virginia. Aeons ago, before continental drift opened up the Atlantic, they formed one system so geologically when you cross the Dyfi you are crossing from Europe to a piece of America, left behind when the continents separated. No wonder they speak differently.
8 The allocation of a single route number (the A470) for the road from Glan Conwy to Cardiff was only made in November 1972, following a campaign in the *Western Mail*.
9 In recent years this quote has been vaguely attributed to several people, including John Redwood. I first heard it in the mid 1960s from an engineer who came from Neath

and if my memory is correct he claimed he had been present at the dinner so I would suggest that Cartwright is a more likely source than Redwood. It was with this anecdote in mind that I was well prepared to make an effective intervention when a previous Permanent Secretary of the Welsh Office asked, in a speech at Gregynog: "And what is the Welsh word for 'Angst'?"

10 See Robert Griffiths, 'The Other Aneurin Bevan', *Planet* No 41, January 1978; and Gwyn Jenkins, 'Keeping Up with the Macs – the Devolution Debate of 1957-59', *Planet* No 82, August 1990.

11 F.M. Cornford, *Microcosmographia Academica – Being a Guide for the Young Academic Politician*, London, 1908, page 26.

12 Lord Griffiths of Fforestfach, *A Conservative Agenda for Wales*, Institute of Welsh Politics Annual Lecture, University of Wales Aberystwyth, November 2002.

13 Eddie Bowen went on to become the inventor of airborne radar. Mitchell, Randall and Bowen were the three individuals who together won the Battle of Britain and hence the war in Europe. In 1940 Churchill entrusted Bowen to go to the USA with a wooden box containing all Britain's main technical secrets, including the first cavity magnetron. Bowen helped set up the Radiation Laboratory, the most spectacularly successful laboratory in the history of science producing in a few years well over a dozen Nobel laureates. After the war Bowen became head of the government Department for Scientific and Industrial Research in Australia and as such he built the famous Parkes radio-telescope – star of the superb film 'The Dish'. He also pioneered the crystal seeding of clouds to produce rain. One of the most important Welshmen of all time and hence almost totally unknown in Wales. Need I add that as well as being a radio astronomer he was a member of Plaid Cymru.

14 See Richard Wyn Jones and Roger Scully, 'Let's Make it Work' in *Agenda*, IWA, Winter 2002/03 for a full analysis of these statistics.

IWA PUBLICATIONS

Agenda
The Institute's regular journal. Appears three times a year.
£5 for a single issue, £15 yearly subscription

Research Reports
The Welsh Potential for Renewable Energy
Edited by Eilidh Johnston. December 2002. £10
An Absolute Duty: Equal Opportunities and the National
Assembly
By Paul Chaney and Ralph Fevre. August 2002. Main report
£20. Summary £5
Competing with the World: Development strategies compared
July 2002. £10
A Guide to European Funding in Wales 2000 – 2006
New edition May 2002. £10
The Third Mission: Creating a Business Culture for Higher
Education in Wales
By Dr. Gareth Jones. April 2002. £10
Tools for the Learning Country December2001. £5
The Search for Balance. Taxing and Spending across the UK
By Ross Mackay. June 2001. £10
Knowledge and the Welsh Economy
By Professor Sir Adrian Webb June 2001. £10
An Icon for Modern Wales:
Realising the Benefits of the National Botanic Garden
By Neil Caldwell & John Stoner February 2001. £10 Main
Report £20

Craft As Art:
Projecting the Makers of Wales Within the Global Economy
by John Osmond February 2001. £10
Beyond the Border: The Acceptability of the WelshBac to
Higher Education

Institutions outside Wales (bilingual)
by Cerian Black & John David Sept ember 2001. £10
The Irish Experience of Objective One
by John Osmond June 2000. £10
Waste in Wales – A National Resource
February 2000 £30, Summary report. £10

Discussion Papers
Divided We Fall: The Politics of Geography in Wales
by John Osmond (November 2002). £5
A Reorganistion Too Far: IWA Response to the National As-
    sembly consultation
document: Structural Change in the NHS in Wales
by Gareth Jones (October 2001). £5
Variable Geometry UK
by Rhodri Morgan AM (March 2000). £5
Funding, Fairness, Farming and the Future
by Professor Gareth Wyn Jones (December 1999) £5
Welsh Politics in the New Millennium
by John Osmond (August 1999) £5

Gregynog Booklets
The Future of Welsh Conservatism
by Jonathan Evans MEP, April 2002. £7.99
Creating an Entrepreneurial Wales
by Professor Dylan Jones-Evans, September 2001. £7.99
Devolution: A Process Not an Event
by Ron Davies MP, February 1999. £7.50

Lectures
The Capital, Culture and the Nation
By Geraint Talfan Davies, National Eisteddfod Lecture
St David's 2002. £7.50
The Role of Universities in the Modern Economy
By Prof Deian Hopkin, National Eisteddfod Lecture
Denbigh 2001. £7.99

Assembly Monitoring
Book publications
Birth of Welsh Democracy
Edited by John Osmond & J Barry Jones March 2003 £19.99
Building a Civic Culture
Edited by J Barry Jones & John Osmond March 2002. £15
Inclusive Government and Party Management
Edited by J Barry Jones and John Osmond March 2001. £15
Quarterly Reports (started December 1999)
Dragon Debates its Future
December 2002 – March 2003 £10
Dragon Takes A Different Route
September – December 2002. £10
A Bilingual Wales
June – August 2002. £10
Engaging with Europe
March – June 2002. £10
Education Policy Breaks Loose
December 2001 – March 2002. £10
Coalition Creaks over Health
September – December 2001. £10

Papers
Developing a Partnership Approach to Primary Legislation
   between Westminster and the National Assembly
By Professor Keith Patchett. Oct 2002. £5
The Future of Welsh Devolution Presentation to the
House of Lords Select Committee on the Constitution
By John Osmond June 2002. £5
Enhancing Welsh Input into Westminster Legislation
by Prof Keith Patchett & John Osmond March 2001. £5
To order please contact the address below. Post & Package
   £1.50 (up to two items) £3 (three or more).
IWA, Ty Oldfield, Llantrisant Road, Llandaf, Cardiff, CF5
   2YQ. Telephone 029 2057 5511 Facsimile 029 2057 5701 Web
   www.iwa.org.uk
Please see our website www.iwa.org.uk for full list of publi-
   cations